YoungWriters® Est. 1991

Little Dreamers
Acrostics

Sparkling Imaginations

Edited By Wendy Laws

First published in Great Britain in 2025 by:

YoungWriters®
Est. 1991

Young Writers
Remus House
Coltsfoot Drive
Peterborough
PE2 9BF
Telephone: 01733 890066
Website: www.youngwriters.co.uk

All Rights Reserved
Book Design by Ashley Janson
© Copyright Contributors 2024
Softback ISBN 978-1-83685-210-0
Printed and bound in the UK by BookPrintingUK
Website: www.bookprintinguk.com
YB0627A

Foreword

Welcome Reader,

For Young Writers' latest competition Little Dreamers, we asked primary school pupils to write an acrostic poem. They could write about an animal, their favourite person, themselves or something from their imagination – anything at all! The acrostic is a fantastic introduction to poetry writing as it comes with a built-in structure, allowing children to focus on their creativity and vocabulary choice.

We live and breathe creativity here at Young Writers and we want to pass our love of the written word onto the next generation – what better way to do that than to celebrate their writing by publishing it in a book!

Featuring poems on a range of topics, this anthology is brimming with imagination and creativity, showcasing the blossoming writing skills of these young poets. They have brought their ideas to life using the power of words, resulting in some brilliant and fun acrostic poems!

Each awesome poet in this book should be super proud of themselves! We hope you will delight in these poems as much as we have.

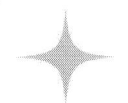

Contents

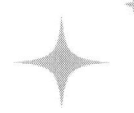

Independent Entrants

Arya Patel (6)	1
Adrian Rimicane (6)	2
Rebecca William (7)	3
Amelia Berentzen (5)	4
Willow McMyn (6)	5
Janujany Srikanth (6)	6
Ibrahim Ahmed (7)	7
Musa Hirst (6)	8
Joshua Otalor (5)	9
Juno Vicary (6)	10
Jenson Chapman (5)	11
Amal Ali (5)	12
Odria Ernstsone (7)	13
Jamal Zaidi (5)	14
Sama Yaqoob (6)	15
Ella Holness (6)	16
Florence Rose Hall (6)	17
Annabel Poppy Turner (7)	18
Mateo Montaque (6)	19
Aliya Mahmood (6)	20
Jasmine Gascoigne-Taylor (7)	21
Harroop Singh (6)	22
Oliver Fields (7)	23
Amber Vallance (7)	24
Noah Dempsey (7)	25
Darasimi Olakunle (5)	26
George Woods-Carrick (5)	27
Mia Ana Ana Rodrigues (5)	28
Jaanki Solanki (6)	29
Ariana Bayati (7)	30
Finley Morton (6)	31
Alfie Boulton (6)	32
Isabell Miller (6)	33
Isabelle Fields (5)	34
Mila Rani Shah (8)	35
Mina Swanzy-Essien (7)	36
Hamza Nawaz (7)	37
Jezrahiah Jabran John (7)	38
Ariya Mistry (6)	39
Anthony Din (5)	40
Eithne Reynolds (7)	41
Haroun Zaizaa (7)	42
Oneli Gallage (5)	43
Matilda Ashmore (6)	44
Mehtaab Dhillon (7)	45
Olivia Poppy (6)	46
Otis Weetman (7)	47
Rebecca Cacula (5)	48
Riyaansini Karthik (5)	49
Vixen-Jupiter Foster (8)	50
Eliza Garland (6)	51
Joseph Mulvihill (5)	52
Vesper Owen (6)	53
Amreet Kaur Basson (6)	54
Muhammad Ayan (5)	55
Finley Ballard (4)	56
Bethany May (6)	57
Faez Kashif (7)	58
Yusuf Parekh (8)	59
Toren Summersgill (6)	60
Eden Wheeler (6)	61
Oluwatumi Adelaja (6)	62
Titilayo Fatusin (4)	63
Martha Lambert (6)	64
Angela Mateen (5)	65
Saoirse Spencer (5)	66
Maira Raheel (5)	67
Leo Simpson	68
Haig	69

Sleep

S leeping in the night, thinking of so many wonderful different dreams. If you take your time and think, they will become better and better.

L ying down in your bed, think about all the wonderful dreams you have in your mind. Imagine you have a pen and paper and slowly write down your different dreams.

E verybody can think about their own dreams. Just think and maybe your dreams could come true.

E njoy the time being in your bed, maybe you could become a magical fairy when you are older.

P retty magical creatures floating around in your head.

Arya Patel (6)

Raindrops

R ain, rain, rain drips all day long,
A dventure starts, as the rain drips a song.
I put on my yellow coat, I open my heart to venture,
N ow I can jump in muddy puddles, sailboats, bake a mud pie,
D own the drain goes the rain, as my misery washes away and boringness flies.
R ain, rain, rain drips all day long,
O h my goodness, the rain singing me a lullaby,
P rance in the middle of July, stars high in the sky.
S pit-spat, pitter-pat, raindrops performing backflips on my windowsill.

Adrian Rimicane (6)

I Dream About A Clean World

W hen she bought a sweetie, she dropped me carelessly on the floor
R ecycling is a good thing he thought to himself, why didn't the girl recycle me?
A lone in the soil, worms choking on me
P olluting the environment, feeling sad. Why did the girl dump me here?
P assing time hour by hour, feeling guilty
E verlasting days and nights. Finally someone picks me up and puts me in the recycling
R ubbish is still out there waiting to be collected by lots of people. Please don't litter the environment.

Rebecca William (7)

Kindness

K indness can spread love all the places you go
I t can make people feel happy and then they might do it to you
N ever make people feel sad or leave them out
D on't ever make people feel like they're not your friend
N o matter what, there's always time to giggle
E verybody is equal so treat them nicely
S ometimes talking can help you feel better when you are sad
S o when people come round, make them a cup of tea and fetch some biscuits!

Amelia Berentzen (5)

Invisibility

I have a superpower
N o one knows yet
V ery likely they never will
I have the superpower of invisibility
S econdly, I steal lots of biscuits
I have a great superpower
B uns and biscuits are good foods to eat
I love munching and crunching on the food
L icking my lips I go downstairs and munch
I love sneaking down and munching on buns
T rying to go and get another biscuit
Y ou need to try a biscuit!

Willow McMyn (6)

In Janurai World

U nicorns are amazing!
N ice little Unicorn Januvi can dance.
I n Janurai World, Janujany cries diamonds but smiles rainbows.
C lever Januvi the Unicorn can talk and sing Janujany to sleep.
O ut of Janujany's sixteen unicorns, Januvi is her favourite.
R eading with Januvi before bedtime makes Janujany really happy.
N ormally, Janujany rides on Januvi and plays with her!
S weet Januvi is like my sister!

Janujany Srikanth (6)

When I Grow Up, I Want To Be A... Cricketer

C entury is 100 runs
R unners, running after batting
I t's a sixer! My team is clapping
C heering fans, jumping for joy
K neeling low, diving fast, to stop the ball at the boundary
E ngland, Three Lions, roaring
T actics secretly whispered, urging players to win
E normous stadiums, bright lights, neat, green grass
R ise of the batsmen and bowlers, all-rounders and cricket champions.

Ibrahim Ahmed (7)

Hedgehog Human

H uman turned into a hedgehog
E yes became smaller than he remembered
D octor couldn't help him to return to the human
G iggle around on the bed in the hospital
E at my hopes and ambitions
H ungry family hedgehogs came to visit him at the hospital
O peration will be completed successfully?
G ratefully I was able to turn back into a human.

Juno Vicary (6)

Treasure Each Other Forever

T reasure everyone in your life,
R emember to be yourself, you are enough.
E veryone deserves to be treasured,
A nd to be loved, cuddled and hugged.
S o always be the one who goes that extra mile,
U s together we care for each other.
R eally believe me,
E ven talking for a while, will make someone smile.

Jenson Chapman (5)

Thunderstorms

T hunder and lightning
H orribly loud
U nder the covers
N ight is cold
D ark skies
E verything is scary
R aining heavily
S udden flash and a bang
T errified
O h no
R un, run, run
M ummy, Mummy I am scared
"S sssss... you are safe now..."

Amal Ali (5)

Scientist

S cientists are smart
C lever and brave
I nventing things that people never made
E very day they make experiments
N ever scared to try something new
T elling people all about the world
I magine what they are doing now
S cientists can tell you many things
T eaching kids all about the world.

Odria Ernstsone (7)

Pumpkin Head

P lease keep it away
U sually playing with my toys
M y vanilla candies
P lease look at the stars
K ids love Pumpkin Head
I like you a lot
N ight-times are scary

H i, Pumpkin Head
E ek, you scared me
A t morning she sleeps
D id you eat your breakfast?

Ella Holness (6)

Heights

H igher and higher I go. What will I find when I come down?
E very step I go through the clouds the Earth feels further away
I 'll climb to the top so I can see the whole world
G rabbing on to calm me down
H eart racing
T rying not to fall when I take a step
S afe and sound as I reach the ground.

Florence Rose Hall (6)

Everyone Should Love Dogs!

D ogs are the best animals because they are very playful, lovely and soft
O r they can be a bit grumpy, mad and might bite you at times
G iraffes are like dogs but just less playful, less helpful and loving
S ometimes dogs can be hurtful and sometimes they can love you very much

You might be strict with your wonderful dog.

Annabel Poppy Turner (7)

Dragons

D ynamic dragons are being outnumbered by predators
R acing against time to survive
A re we there yet or are we behind?
G o, go, go! As fast as you can
O h no, no, no! It's too dangerous down there
N o! Just go, they're catching up now
S o their lives are saved, my dream has ended.

Mateo Montaque (6)

Winter Kitten

W andering alone
I n the cold
N ext to my house
T hrough the window
E ating the snow
R unning around

K itten
I like you
T hank you for coming
T aking all the cat food
E very piece I left for you
N o one else cares but I do.

Aliya Mahmood (6)

Fairy Land

F rolicking about like a dancer
A lways kind and caring
I n positive moods
R ainbow in her heart
Y et her magic is as loving as a smile

L ight and sparkly like a star
A lmost like a diamond
N ot just an ordinary mushroom
D ancing with life.

Jasmine Gascoigne-Taylor (7)

Disneyland

D isneyland is a palace
I dream about going to see the princesses
S now White is the sweetest princess
N ice and colourful
E lsa will dance
Y ummy food
L ots of fun
A nna is a summer princess
N ever-ending fun
D reams do come true.

Harroop Singh (6)

Adventurer

A dventures at the ready
D aring to be brave
V enturing far and wide
E agle-eyed and carefree
N ot stopping for anyone
T esting myself to the limits
U sing all my might
R eaching the limits to the
E ternal end
R eady to go? I am!

Oliver Fields (7)

Fabulous

F lowers make you happy
A nd friends can make everyone laugh
B abies are cute, so are you
U nder an umbrella you are clean
L ove is important
O nly onions should make you cry
U nicorns make you excited
S tars are bright, they make the sky magical.

Amber Vallance (7)

Football

F ootball is my favourite sport
O n the green grass
O r on the slippery AstroTurf
T ackle, save, dribble in defence
B e ready to receive the ball
A ll the players in a team
L ots of passing and scoring goals in a team
L ots of fun for everyone.

Noah Dempsey (7)

Abu Dhabi

A lovely desert safari
B eautiful beaches for summer
U nbelievable inventions

D esert as far as I can see
H aving the tallest buildings in the world
A rabic is the local language
B rilliant waterparks and theme parks
I love Abu Dhabi.

Darasimi Olakunle (5)

My Friends

M y friends are great
Y oghurts we like to eat

F urchester Hotel we like to see
R unning is fun together
I love my friends
E ating tagliatelle with my friends
N aughty friends are stinky
D inosaurs go roar
S uper friends.

George Woods-Carrick (5)

Summertime

S unshine's
U p in the sky
M akes me hot
M akes me thirsty
E agles fly up in the sky
R ain comes when the sun is gone
T ime to play
I n the sand
M aking lots of parties, fun and
E ating lots of ice cream.

Mia Ana Ana Rodrigues (5)

Halloween Poem

H earing spooky sounds
A ll around are ghosts
L urking around are vampires
L ots of spiderwebs
O h, so scary
W itches are cackling
E ating eyeballs and blood
E vil zombies walking
N aughty bats flying.

Jaanki Solanki (6)

Sheepdog

S trong, powerful legs
H elpful to farmers
E legantly, jumps over fences
E choing loud bark
P ouncing around the sheep
D irecting the runaway sheep
O ver the fence and into the pens
G alloping home to his master.

Ariana Bayati (7)

I Love Cats

I ncredible, so adorable

L oving pets
O ver the fence, they jump
V elvet fur
E nergetic and playful

C uddly and cute
A ll different colours
T iny, adorable kittens
S uper scratchers.

Finley Morton (6)

Explorer

E xploring is dangerous
X is where the treasure is
P lease pack your bag
L ight your campfire
O r it will get dark and cold
R emember to bring your tent
E xtra food and marshmallows for a
R eally big feast.

Alfie Boulton (6)

Dinner Lady

D inner lady
I choose my spot
N ext to my friend
N o teachers allowed
E ager to eat
R umbling tummy

L asagne on my plate
A nd my water bottle
D essert is next
Y ummy, yummy!

Isabell Miller (6)

Unicorn

U nbelievable to some
N ot to me, they are
I ncredible and beautiful
C olourful and magical
O n rainbows they ride
R unning through the meadows
N ow they must rest
S afe in my wonderful bed of dreams.

Isabelle Fields (5)

Scientist

S cience is cool
C hemistry is involved
I nteresting experiments
E xcellent discoveries
N ew answers every day
T oo many explosions
I nformative sheets
S uper team
T ogether we can do it.

Mila Rani Shah (8)

Invisible

I n a state of despair
N ever seen
V icious people abandon me
I gnored
S orrow
I n a luminous city filled with lights
B right lights fill the night
L onely
E very lonely day is the same.

Mina Swanzy-Essien (7)

Engineer

E ngineering is my dream
N ever give up
G reat at solving problems
I magine all the things we can make
N ew ideas every day
E ducation is the key
E ndless ideas
R each high and achieve your dreams.

Hamza Nawaz (7)

Star Wars

S tar Wars
T hey are so tough
A nd highly trained troops anywhere
R evive from everywhere

W hy do they wear heavy suits?
A ctually, I don't know
R azor-sharp knife
S o they survive.

Jezrahiah Jabran John (7)

Diwali

D iwali is about good over evil.
I t comes when the new moon is near.
W e make rangolis using bright colours.
A ll friends and family come together,
L ighting diyas and fireworks.
I love this festival of lights!

Ariya Mistry (6)

I Dream Of Spiders

S piders hiding in my socks
P lease don't bite me
I will shout
D angerous but I am fearless
E very web is sticky and shiny
R ocks are better than my socks to hide
S pider-Man is that you?

Anthony Din (5)

Friends

F riends are the best
R ocking good times
I love my friends so much
E verybody has a special friend
N ever lets you down
D o you want to play with me?
S uper days ahead for you and me.

Eithne Reynolds (7)

I Want To Be A Builder

B uilding houses
U nite family
I t's awesome
L et's build together
D oors, walls and windows
I magination at play
N ew memories every day
G rowing love in every way.

Haroun Zaizaa (7)

Superhero

S o smart my daddy
U p high in the sky
P rotecting me
E very night dreaming
R eally good
H e is in heaven
E very day makes me happy
R ead my mind
O bviously.

Oneli Gallage (5)

Flowers

F antastic flowers
L ovely smells
O xygen made to help our environment
W ater helps them grow
E xciting colours
R oots growing under the soil
S unny days make flowers grow tall.

Matilda Ashmore (6)

Teacher

T eachers help students
E very day, they teach us the work
A lways caring and sweet
C lever and smart
H elpful and kind
E ven when we are stuck
R eally amazing and the best!

Mehtaab Dhillon (7)

Flowers

F lowers are beautiful
L ovely to look at
O n a table or in the garden
W e love to see them
E veryone loves flowers
R ed ones are my favourite
S melling them makes me happy.

Olivia Poppy (6)

Tractor

T he tractor chugs a lot
R ound and round the wheels go
A cross the fields
C ombine and tractor work together
T owing a trailer of wheat
O n the farm
R eady to make bread.

Otis Weetman (7)

Rebecca

R eally nice and kind
E nsuring everyone is fine
B eautiful mind
E ach day searching for fun
C lever and smart
C ares about everyone
A lways there for family and friends.

Rebecca Cacula (5)

Rainbow

R efraction
A n incredible multicoloured circular
I nternal reflection
N ot just one colour
B eauty and harmony
O ptical phenomenon
W ith different and amazing colours.

Riyaansini Karthik (5)

Autumn

A corns fall off the trees
U mbrellas flow in the breeze
T oasting marshmallows on a fire
U nder the stars in cosy attire
M ushrooms growing from the ground
N ature is all around

Vixen-Jupiter Foster (8)

Family

F amily is my favourite thing
A ll my family are amazing
M e and my family love each other
I love my family
L ove is all a family needs
Y ou are never alone with family.

Eliza Garland (6)

Holiday

H appy times to be had
O n this holiday
L ots of joy
I nteresting insects to see
D ays of sun and salty sea
A way I sail on my boat
Y ou would love it too.

Joseph Mulvihill (5)

Pandy Cat

P retty cat
A nd
N ice
D ances all the time
Y ellow flowers are his favourite

C uddles and hug attacks
A mazing at flips
T otally fun.

Vesper Owen (6)

Flowers

F lowers bloom out at me
L ovely to look at
O h some so tall
W ow! So colourful
E very flower is unique
R oses are red
S o beautiful all of them are.

Amreet Kaur Basson (6)

School Is So Hard!

S tudying is hard
C ool recess is better
H ate homework so much
O of, it is so tiring
O ops, time for class again
L earning can be tough.

Muhammad Ayan (5)

Stars

S tars shining in the sky
P lanets spinning round and round
A stronauts floating
C omets blasting through space
E arth is the planet where we live.

Finley Ballard (4)

Penguins

P enguins waddle
E ggs warming
N ests ready
G old markings show
U nderwater swimming
I ce and snow
N ew penguins playing.

Bethany May (6)

Beach

B lue waves are at the beach
E els and fish under the sea
A castle made of sand
C olour for kites in the sky
H appy memories last forever.

Faez Kashif (7)

Football

F ootball
O ut of the goal
O bstacle and people
T raining
B all
A way
L oss in match
L eg.

Yusuf Parekh (8)

Minecraft

M ob
I ron
N oob
E at bread
C reeper
R eally fun
A xolotl
F ish
T rees.

Toren Summersgill (6)

Archie

A new puppy in the house
R eally cute
C hocolate coloured
H appy dog
I nto everything
E xhausted.

Eden Wheeler (6)

Singer

S ong
I nstrument
N ot being scared
G et the microphone ready
E verybody looking at me
R ehearsal.

Oluwatumi Adelaja (6)

Sister, Baby Sister

S ister, baby sister
I love you
S leepyhead
T emidayo, Temi
E at, eat, eat
R eally sweet

Titilayo Fatusin (4)

Koala

K oalas are cuddly
O n trees hanging
A re very sluggish
L arge round head
A round nature.

Martha Lambert (6)

Castle

C olourful ones
A re old
S andcastle
T all ones
L ittle princess
E mpty ones.

Angela Mateen (5)

Going To The Fair

F unny clowns make people laugh
A crobats people amaze
I t's terrific
R ides are fun.

Saoirse Spencer (5)

My Tiger Acrostic Poem

T igers
I n the woods
G rowling at others
E veryone is scared
R un away!

Maira Raheel (5)

Dack The Monster

D oes football
A lways glows in the dark
C old
K ind and really loves Miss Morgan.

Leo Simpson

Haig

H appy
A lways hungry
I n a cave, he lives
G reen.

Haig

I Dream About...

I dream about going to a zoo

D inosaurs are growling
R ain is dropping
E lephants are trumpeting
A pples are dropping from a tree
M onkeys are swinging

A pples growing on apple trees
B asketball people are playing
O striches are running
U mbrellas in case it rains
T igers are growling.

Nefeli Koudounis (5)
John Ball Primary School, Blackheath

Lewandowski

L et's go!
E nergy and speed are some things that we need
W inning always feels good
A s we play we get better
N ever give up
D reamwork, teamwork
O ffside stops the game
W e are always good players
S occer means football in the USA
K eep the ball safe from others
I would love to play with him.

Jan Downar-Zapolski (7)
John Ball Primary School, Blackheath

Autumn Day

A ll day the leaves fell
U nder the conker tree.
T he trees blew with the squirrels
U nderneath, storing conkers.
M illions of conkers fell
N ear the squirrels' den, then a

D angerous animal came
A nd took some of the
Y ellow and brown conkers.

Elliot Lewis-Bowler (7)
John Ball Primary School, Blackheath

Christmas

C andy canes,
H appy feelings,
R eindeer rides.
I ce and snow, everywhere we go,
S lippy pavements, watch your step!
T he magic Santa sends through the year
M akes everybody happy here.
A s soon as Christmas arrives,
S nowball fun and children smile.

Artie Ivanovitch (6)
John Ball Primary School, Blackheath

Designer

D angerous to sew when you're five
E xcited to be a designer
S o eager to be a designer
I deas of dresses
G rowing up to be a designer
N ervous to be a designer
E ager to be a designer
R ight! I'm starting to sew now.

Phoebe Lyth (6)
John Ball Primary School, Blackheath

Teacher

T eachers teach me many things
E very teacher makes me happy
A ll the teachers are kind and helpful
C heers, thank you to my teachers
"**H** ello teacher, I am here"
E very morning I say to her
R eading books she teaches me.

Gesu Gulamadshoeva (6)
John Ball Primary School, Blackheath

Horse Rider

H orses are fast
O n a morning jog
R un through the field
S unshine
E xtremely sunny

R un through the pitch
I ndoor running
D own the hill
E very horse is fast
R acing fast.

Mila Nichter (5)
John Ball Primary School, Blackheath

Insects

I nsects make me fear
N ow when they come near me
S ay, "Oh no," and run away
E quality, let's keep us apart
C ome near me, friends, help me now!
T ry to get away from it
S ure, am I safe now?

Beatrice Cheung (6)
John Ball Primary School, Blackheath

Astronaut

A stronauts floating
S hooting stars
T ime for take-off
R ocket's ready
O n the moon
N o gravity
A nother star
U gly aliens, going to space high in the sky
T errific time.

Sofia Kalamchi (5)
John Ball Primary School, Blackheath

Ballerina

B allet dancing
A pink dress
L ove dancing
L ove the music
E verybody's excellent in ballet
R emember the moves
I am good at ballet
N ever give up
A big talent.

Maybelle Sutton (5)
John Ball Primary School, Blackheath

Halloween

H appy Halloween
A bat flew out its wing
L ittle witches fly
L aughing with might
O wls fly away in fright
W ishy witch
E vil eye
E very night is creepy
N ight flies.

Mia Message (6)
John Ball Primary School, Blackheath

Footballer

F ast running
O n the bench
O n the chair
T aking a penalty
B all in the goal
A kicking kick
L ots of goals
L ots of players
E nd result
R oaring crowds.

Leno Giquel (5)
John Ball Primary School, Blackheath

Piano

P eople love to do it and yes
I t's simple and easy, they love it
A nd I'm very good, it is true
N o one hates it and it's peaceful
O nce you try it, it blows your heart away because it is so fun.

Elliot Rothlisberger (7)
John Ball Primary School, Blackheath

Footballer

F ast feet
O ver the bar
O n the penalty spot
T ackling
B ig goals
A round the pitch
L ovely calls
L ots of balls
E veryone is having fun
R unning fast.

Mislav Murray (5)
John Ball Primary School, Blackheath

Ballerina

B allet shoes
A beautiful dancer
L earning to bounce
L ive to dance
E njoying the dance
R emember the moves
I n my tutu
N ever give up
A t the dance studio.

Boè Bushnell (5)
John Ball Primary School, Blackheath

Teacher

T eachers are good because they teach you to learn
E ven they always teach you
A nyone can learn from them
C an you do this?
H elp people
E veryone can learn and play
R ead books.

Lily Mandlik-Smith (5)
John Ball Primary School, Blackheath

Footballer

F ootball player
O n the pitch
O ne-nil
T eam
B all
A ttacking tackling
L ove football
L oser
E veryone squeals
R eferee.

Xyan Pusey (5)
John Ball Primary School, Blackheath

Plane

P lanes carry passengers abroad
L anding is the most exciting part
A re you ready to go through the clouds?
N ight sleep is so relaxing
E veryone have a great plane journey!

Altan Korkmaz (6)
John Ball Primary School, Blackheath

Spiders

S piders scuttle around
P eople are sometimes scared of them
I am not
D ark corners on the wall
E nemy for some people
R un around
S cary and hairy.

Orlanda Storrs Farr (7)
John Ball Primary School, Blackheath

Scientist

S uper
C razy
I deas
E xplosions
N ight glow explosions
T iny science about bugs
I cy slime
S cary science bugs
T iny bugs.

Matulino Asi Pito (6)
John Ball Primary School, Blackheath

Scientist

S cience
C hemicals
I nvestigation
E xperiment
N ew discovery
T ests
I mportant work
S cience lab
T ime to get to work.

Erin-Mei Lynam (5)
John Ball Primary School, Blackheath

Shark

S harks scare me
"**H** urry! Run!" Harry shouted at me
"**A** rgh! The shark bit me
R ight here! Help me!
K eep pulling me out or I will die!"

Eli Lum (6)
John Ball Primary School, Blackheath

Builder

B uilding blocks
U nder the roof
I am fixing rooms
L emon juice
D oing and building the walls
E very day I build
R aining inside.

Khalil Broughton (6)
John Ball Primary School, Blackheath

Builder

B uilding is what you do
U nder houses
I can fix things
L ots of jobs
D rinking some juice
E arly mornings
R unning for the job.

Roman Komarov (6)
John Ball Primary School, Blackheath

Rocket

R ockets are big
O h, and they go into space
C lip your seatbelt
K ick the accelerator
E ngine is powered up
T ake off and zoom into space!

Rohan Mehrotra (6)
John Ball Primary School, Blackheath

Football

F ootball
O n the bench
O ver the wall
T eam training
B all in the goal
A nother goal
L ots of goals
L ots of fun.

Jamie John-Phillip (5)
John Ball Primary School, Blackheath

When I Grow Up I Want To Be A Dentist

D on't worry
E nd of your pain
N o tooth decay
T eeth are good
I 've nearly finished
S o easy
T eeth are healthy now.

Inas Ali (6)
John Ball Primary School, Blackheath

Gymnastics

G irl
Y ay
M akes me happy
N ervous
A ctive
S ome
T ap
I n
C lass
S ame again.

Viktoriia Kharevych (5)
John Ball Primary School, Blackheath

Mermaid

M y tail
E specially pink
R ice
M y mum is awesome
A nts at a picnic
I love my mum
D o not get damp.

Sofia Fusi Shaw (5)
John Ball Primary School, Blackheath

Police

P olice help people
O fficer
L ots of people to help
I n their uniform
C atch bad guys
E veryone is safe.

Dabira Abiodun (5)
John Ball Primary School, Blackheath

Scooters

S cootering
C ars
O h I love cars
O h I love to be at
T he park with Ariel
E njoyable
R aces.

Reema Fayiz (5)
John Ball Primary School, Blackheath

Singer

S ound
I have a good voice
N ever give up
G ood singing
E lephants can't sing
R ocking music songs.

Freddie Ryan (5)
John Ball Primary School, Blackheath

Spring

S pring is fun
P ink leaves
R ed leaves
I t is fun
N ow I love spring
G o and see the bunnies hopping.

Nina Mevarach (5)
John Ball Primary School, Blackheath

Designer

D og
E lephant
S nail
I ce cream
'G ator
N et
E gg
R oom.

Alaska Adams (6)
John Ball Primary School, Blackheath

Doctor

D octors help
O n call
C all the doctor
T ake medicine
O ffer help
R eady to help.

Karter Smith (5)
John Ball Primary School, Blackheath

Teacher

T eaching
E xcellent
A lways
C lassroom
H appy
E xceptional
R emember.

Thea Abram (5)
John Ball Primary School, Blackheath

Ballet

B right lights
A big show
L eaping
L ights shining
E xercise
T reat at the pub.

Vivien M (5)
John Ball Primary School, Blackheath

Stars

S tars
T he sky is clean
A re stars bright?
R eally high up in the sky
S tars are lovely.

Arius Lleshaj (5)
John Ball Primary School, Blackheath

Train

T rain on the tracks
R eally fast
A lot of passengers
I love trains
N ow at the garage.

Akin Korkmaz (5)
John Ball Primary School, Blackheath

Singer

S uper good
I ncredible
N ervous
G ood singer
E xtra good
R ock music.

Kyrie Dajan (5)
John Ball Primary School, Blackheath

Because

B ig
E lephant
C at
A ct
U mbrella
S nake
E pic.

Ada Evrenos (6)
John Ball Primary School, Blackheath

Power

P ower
O strich speed
W ater power
E at more food
R ush to the power.

Callie Bell (6)
John Ball Primary School, Blackheath

Rugby

R unning fast
U nder the lights
G o fast
B e kind
Y ou can do it.

Alistair Macdonald (5)
John Ball Primary School, Blackheath

Police

P lease people
O range
L ollipops
I n
C at
E lephant.

Zofia Wojda (5)
John Ball Primary School, Blackheath

Friend

F riend
R at
I ce
E pic
N an
D ad
S ad.

Hayden (5)
John Ball Primary School, Blackheath

Police

P erson
O cean
L ollipop
I ce
C at
E gg.

Raheem-Khalil Latham (5)
John Ball Primary School, Blackheath

Dig

D inosaur bones
I n the ground
G etting dug up.

Rufus Johnson (5)
John Ball Primary School, Blackheath

Young Writers Information

We hope you have enjoyed reading this book – and that you will continue to in the coming years.

If you're the parent or family member of an enthusiastic poet or story writer, do visit our website **www.youngwriters.co.uk/subscribe** and sign up to receive news, competitions, writing challenges and tips, activities and much, much more! There's lots to keep budding writers motivated!

If you would like to order further copies of this book, or any of our other titles, then please give us a call or order via your online account.

Young Writers
Remus House
Coltsfoot Drive
Peterborough
PE2 9BF
(01733) 890066
info@youngwriters.co.uk

**Join in the conversation!
Tips, news, giveaways and much more!**

YoungWritersUK   YoungWritersCW   youngwriterscw

youngwriterscw   youngwriterscw-uk